"Lisa is one of my favourit
now… check her poetry out."

"Thought-provoking and joyful: Lockdown laid out poignantly, humanely, tenderly, playfully."

"Lisa's work is powerful and inspiring; always on the pulse of current events and shaking her readers from stupor, demanding that we stare at the world and fight for it."

"Lisa's work has kept us going through lockdown life. She has captured the many feelings and fears we all had, the ones that keep us awake at night wondering if we will ever be 'normal again'. She has captured this moment in history in her beautiful, unique way"

LOCKDOWN LIFE
A ROLLERCOASTER OF EMOTIONS

LISA O'HARE

MASTER HOUSE PUBLISHING

First Edition published in the United Kingdom in 2021 by
Master House Publishing Ltd
www.masterhousepublishing.com

ISBN: 978-1-8384829-1-6

Lockdown Life, A Rollercoaster Of Emotions
© 2021 Lisa O'Hare
www.lisaoharewriter.com

A CIP catalogue record for this book is available from the British
Library

For Author readings, appearances, speaking event and spoken
word bookings at Colleges, Organisations & Institutions please
use the contact details on the website.

Text Copyright: Lisa O'Hare
Book cover: Self-portrait by Lisa O'Hare ©2021
Cover design: Master House Publishing ©2021
Author photo: Marni V Photography via Lockdown FaceTime
photoshoot.

LOCKDOWN LIFE
A ROLLERCOASTER OF EMOTIONS

LISA O'HARE

MASTER HOUSE
Publishing

LISA O'HARE

This book is dedicated to the people who helped us all to cling on to hope since March 2020. The care workers, nurses, doctors, pharmacists, shop workers, distribution workers, delivery drivers, postal workers, all essential workers keeping the country running, the vaccine scientists, community volunteers, and anyone who helped anyone in even the smallest of ways during this time.

It is also dedicated to all the creative and online connections that supported me during lockdown, whether on social media or on zoom open mics and workshops. I cannot imagine surviving lockdown the same without us all looking out for each other and pushing each other through to the other side of 'all this'.

And obviously my family and friends as who gets a book published and doesn't say thank you to the most important people in their life?

Thank you – you are all ace.

Contents

Preface..15

PART ONE - Reflections of lockdown life

Lockdown Life: A Rollercoaster of Emotions.......19

An ode to the goats of Llandudno..........................21

Nonet for a world leader.......................................23

Lockdown Birthday 24

Poems do not belong in boxes..........................25

Mole whacking 26

Days indistinguishable 28

Lockdown Writers Block......................................29

Lockdown Sunday Blues 30

Quarantine Halloween 31

Calculating the R of Common Sense 32

A Poem for Christmas 2020..................................34

Lockdown Valentines...35

Shame...36

Lockdown Friendship 37

2020 Found in my Instagram captions 38

PART TWO - Lockdown protest poems

Lockdown Protest 43

I'm sorry if you feel 44

Born Free...45

Fears for Tiers 46

Let the record show..47

Phone Atonement 48

Omission 50

To the women...52

Hastags 53

The death of decency..54

PART THREE - Haikus

Pride Haiku..59

Confidence Haiku. 61

PART FOUR - Lockdown Acrostics

FaceTime...65

News 66

Stay Alert..67

Slogan...68

Yachts & planes 69

Anger...70

Systemic 71

Silence 72

Osmosis 73

USA 74

Home 75

Women... 76

Kindness... 77

Bullying 78

Viable... 79

Tiers 80

About The Author...................................….....83

Credits...…...85

Preface

In March 2020, the United Kingdom went into lockdown. Eventually. In the days, months and year that passed, I took to my notepad and keyboard to capture my rollercoasting emotions throughout this time.

From outrage and despair to boredom and sadness; occasionally I let myself or should say *forced* myself to hope. Often all in the same day.

It was a relentless and arduous time. This collection captures how I, along with I am sure so many of us, felt on certain days.

2020 and early 2021 also saw a lot of unrest in society as a whole and protest became a regular feature of this strangest of years. This collection touches on a range of reactions to these moments through poetry and what I call my 'angry acrostics'.

PART ONE
Reflections on lockdown life

A short collection of poems written in response to adjusting to life in lockdown and reacting to both personal and world events that happened during this time.

Lockdown Life, A Rollercoaster of Emotions

It started with confusion
We weren't locking down
We had no time for this viral intrusion
So, we carried on regardless
Which, with hindsight, was a ridiculous act of
delusion.

Then came fear
The rules were strict, yet vague
We had to adhere
How long for?
It was all far from clear
Days blurred into weeks
And by May, well, it felt like a different year.

We could no longer hug
Just like that
Pulled away from us
Like a rug we hadn't even noticed was there.

Each visit online felt like an attack
But not everything we saw was a fact
People would bluster, shout, argue and overreact.

Then came overload
At the never-ending news
Too much to process, too much to download.
I hit mute, mute, mute,
And slowed.

Slowed and retreated
I ran away, at home.
With cooking, books and art

Busy busy busy
Just trying not to fall apart.

And finally came hope
Faith in others keeping us safe,
Those who try to collaborate, educate, elevate.

Hope is not *all* we have
But it helps
So, I hold it tight
As it is all I can hold
Until we can all hold each other again.

An ode to the goats of Llandudno

Seagulls eating deep fried chips and doughnuts
Was the first sign
Swooping our bites straight from our mouths and
hands
Was the next.

We shook our fists to the skies
As they flew over the Great Orme
With their deep-fried prizes.

The goats watched on
In awe at the audacity of their winged friends
Thinking their bravery was boundless
The two legged and the machines with wheels were
terrifying
So, they stuck to their patch
Self-isolating to protect themselves.

From afar they heard the arcades, Punch and Judy
and endless shouting at seagulls at closing time,
The noise overwhelming them, they studiously kept
their distance.

Until....
Closing time stopped
The arcades shutters came down,
The wheeled machines and two legged retreated
The goats bleated

They edged hoof by tentative hoof down the Orme.
Could it be so? Do goat dreams come true?
They ran looking for all the delights they knew their
seagull friends had experienced before them,

The two legged holding up rectangles behind glass
The goats were able to exercise outside their homes
And they reveled in it
More space than ever before
It felt vast,
No longer limited to their territory of grass.

And that joy?
The joy of the goats running wild in Llandudno
Is what we now crave too.

Nonet for a world leader

An internal light insertion
Orifices unspecified
Disinfectant injections
Test if the virus dies.

It was sarcasm
He later lied.

Medical
Doctors
Cried.

Lockdown Birthday

I'm two birthdays a hand wash girl these days,
Of course, we all are
'Happy birthday. Twice'
A piece of trusted government advice.
I chose the Stevie Wonder version,
As an additional precaution.
Wanting to see my next birthday.
And I've made it!
Today I have more candles than cake
No one to hug or even offer a handshake,
Such a shame too
As they are SO CLEAN.
Happy birthday to me.

Poems do not belong in boxes

*Dedicated to the lifeline of open mic poetry on zoom in
lockdown*

Poems do not belong in boxes
But, for now, that is where they're shared.

Assuming the WiFi stays stable
We laugh, rage, and reflect
For as long as we are able.

Missing our homes of pubs and cafes
We stay home to hear what others have to say,
And how they say it, how they see it
We see each other through.

But our poems do not belong in boxes
And one day they'll be set free,
The day the poets meet again
All this, will be history.

Mole whacking

I know this may not be something you want to hear,
But when you whack a mole
Well, the thing is, it doesn't just disappear.

Hear me out on this, but it moves
Over there
Or there... or there
They are basically impossible to control.
So, the analogy doesn't work
You know, about the mole.

We need to be thinking more about damage control,
So maybe, let's not say that again
Let's go with something a bit more...
How do I put this?
Humane.

I know you love a good catchphrase,
To thump your fist to
Like track and trace
Or was tasting and telling?
Tracing, testing, tracking, tasting
Let's call the whole thing off!

So maybe, keep it simple
Keep it straight,
But don't you dare go blaming this on people's
weight!

My suggestion if you want a phrase to win,
No no no, we are not bringing back "take it on the
chin."
And don't throw scientists under the bus

People will see through that
What you need to do takes guts.
And it starts with a "sorry"
And it must be sincere,
After all we have been through, it's the least we
deserve,
It's been a hell of a year.

It's not a performance
You're a real head of state
What you say must be more than just click bait.

So, drop the 'slogan as policy' policy
Not 'it will all be over by Christmas' prophecies.

We *need* you to do better
No, I really don't think you need to send us all
another letter.

It's just if you get better at this
We may start to believe we can get out of this abyss,
As for better or worse
You're the one charged with keeping us all of a
hearse.

NO! Please do not use that!
That would be perverse!

Oh god. He loves it.

I quit.

Days indistinguishable

Days indistinguishable
Except for changes in rules
Until this virus is extinguishable.

Wake Zoom Sleep Repeat
Bin collection day separates the weeks.

But I notice the same tree
On my daily walk,
How it was green, then bloomed
Then green, now golden brown.

It reminds me the world still spins
And we are lucky,
To notice the change in seasons
As we cling on
Waiting for the return of distinguishable days.

Lockdown Writers Block

I can't write
Right now

Words fail me
For now

They'll come back
Some day
Some how

But for today
And for some time to come
I will just have to allow
Them to take a break
Like a holiday
I cannot take.

Right now

All I can do
Is countdown
To the day I can join my words again
On holiday, or wherever they went
Whilst I was locked down.

Lockdown Sunday Blues

My Sunday night fear
Is filled with an unanswerable question
I know I must face
As others will too.

A question well intentioned
But seemingly unaware
That this is tough, relentless and exhausting.

Especially after I couldn't sleep
Wondering what I will say,
When they ask on Zoom at 9am
'Did everyone have a good weekend?'

Quarantine Halloween

2020 is all trick and no treats
No wins, just defeat after defeat.
A year so relentless, restless, and mean
Every day feels like Halloween.

Normality a ghost
Nothing the same, just almost
We wear masks all year
Switching on the news for our fix of the Fear.

Every day feels like a repeat
We are more than overdue a treat
But we need more than Amazon to knock on the door
We need joy and fun, need our spirits to soar.

So, we'll wear costumes at home
Watch scary movies alone,
Hoping to suppress the surge
As we stay home watching 'The Purge'

Bob for apples
In buckets for one,
The faces carved into our pumpkins
Will be second to none.

We'll make the best
Of this scariest of Halloween's,
The one where we are all quarantined.

Calculating the R of Common Sense

Common sense is the X of your intelligence over the
Y of your dense
A delicate balancing act, heavily influenced by those
who like to dispense.
Shady theories from Facebook or YouTube
Or aging rock stars forming new splinter groups
But now when they say 'D'ya know what I mean?'
You get the F.E.A.R. common sense was never in
their baggy jeans,
They should stay there and sit in their Rockin' Chairs
And maybe stay out of public health affairs.

Common sense shoots grouse
Near Barnard Castle,
Common sense has a second house
Also, near Barnard Castle,
Common sense got Brexit done
It made it oven ready,
Common sense hid in a fridge
We all saw that on the telly.

Common sense is in the 'MSM'
But have you read a paper?
'Use your common sense!' they scream
'But not like that!' you traitor!

Common sense cannot be taught
It has no definition
Yet here it is 'our best hope'
To put this virus in remission.
Common sense is the X of intelligence
Over the Y of your dense,
And I fear the former is in short supply

Judging by recent events.

So how to increase supply of common sense
It's R, it's reproduction,
How to convince those anti-masks
Those hell bent on destruction.

I'm really sorry
I just don't know
I haven't got that cracked,
So, its fingers crossed, and all the best
Good luck to trace and track!

A Poem for Christmas 2020

The emergency chair remains folded in the shed
And this year it stays a sofa, not a bed.

If it wasn't for Top of the Pops
And presents of socks,
Would we know it's Christmas time at all?

But we can still binge eat and up our cholesterol,
As we switch between different zoom and phone
calls.

Last Christmas feels so long ago,
I wonder would we have treasured it more
If we knew then
What we now know?

But this year to save us from tiers
Glasses of bubbles will be raised in our small bubbles
As we say 'cheers!'

It's easy to feel like that waitresses song
'I think I'll miss this one this year'
But we will persevere.
So even if it feels lonely this Christmas
We just need to remember
That, this too, shall pass.

Lockdown Valentines

Was Rihanna's place this hopeless?
She found love
She told us
But can love find love
To meet eyes
That give us butterflies

Where does love go
When sliding doors stop
And we're all stuck behind laptops
Losing memories of how it feels to embrace
Dreaming of somewhere
As hopeless as Rhianna's place.

Shame

I carry a shame
So unspeakable it has no name,
No support group
No cure can tame.

Only myself to blame
For all the time it stole
Sometimes draining my entire soul.

It started as fun
Now I am in whole
As I scroll and scroll.

Double tap
Double tap
The phone has me trapped.

Lockdown Friendship

We have never met
But still connect.
Online, given, y'know....

Pandemic.

Something clicked
Just sort of
Alchemic.

2020 Found in my Instagram captions

Old scrapbook memories
Sugar rush leaps off the page
'Tippex is the tool of liars!'
The only motto you'll ever need.

Saw the type of band who wouldn't let you miss your
train,
Music is colour, shade, explosions & joy
Transformative and makes everyone sparkle together
For a moment.

Finding it hard to focus
Feedback from humans outside my head
Would be really helpful
Had some feelings
And nearly made a coffee in a glass instead of a mug.

My productivity is simply a best attempt at distraction
It means nothing,
Just distracting and relaxing
'Distraxing.'

Taking socially distanced walk on the wild side
When life hand you lemons...
Stick a bit of an egg box on your TV and make your
own pyramid stage,
Missed you more Manchester
Memories of a no filter day
2020. Is. Unreal.

PART TWO
Lockdown protest poems

As we were locked down there seemed to be an avalanche of issues that demanded protest and change. From the PPE shortages, to lack of care home protection. The shocking footage of George Floyds murder and ensuing Black Lives Matter protests both in the USA and the UK, school meals scandals, nurses pay, violence against women... the list felt endless and exhausting.

But there was always collective strength and decency to be found. Decency never dies.

Lockdown Protest

I'd protest
But I can't go out
I don't want to do more harm
So, I shout at my TV
Thump my keyboard
When faced with nightly smarm
Behind podiums
And slogans
Intended to disarm
But cause me
Fury and rage
And unrelenting alarm
But I'd protest
If I could go out
And save people from harm.

I'm sorry if you feel

I'm sorry if you feel
You haven't let us down
I'm sorry if you feel
These questions aren't for you
I'm sorry if you feel
Now is not the time
I'm sorry if you feel
Unprecedented is an excuse
I'm sorry if you feel
My fear is not real
I'm sorry if you feel
You've just been following the science
I'm sorry if you feel
It's uncomfortable to mourn the dead
I'm sorry if you feel
I'm sorry you don't feel
Feel empathy
Sorrow
Or shame.

Born Free

'Born free and equal in dignity and rights'
They are the words the declaration cites,
From 1948 to learn lessons from the war
Here, in the 2020s, we must hold on to what
those words were for.

Those rights are for all who are human
We must never let them disappear
                                   an illusion,
Just out of grasp, of those who most need them.

Born free should be a guarantee
Not restricted by others who want you to be,
Different to you
Or the same as to them
For that is not free
That is not Liberty
Dignity for all, leaves no room for such bigotry.

By 2020 this should all just be basics
It really should not still be this complicated
But that is not always the case
Be it gender, religion, or race,
Protecting ourselves and others is a constant
challenge we face.

So always remember these rights are for them
And for you
And for me,
That these rights, when working,
Are what keeps us free.

Fears for Tiers

My fears for these tiers
Is that they save certain but hurt far more other
careers,
That the pain will be felt for years
That requests for support will fall on deaf ears.

Not everybody wants to rule the world
But it seems that those that do, just don't have a
clue
So, we need to shout shout
Until we understand what this is all about

This isn't kind of funny
I find it kind of sad
2020
It's a mad world

Let the record show

Let the record show
Our enquires, reports and commissions
Let the record show
We will 'learn' but provide few admissions
Of shame, regret, or sorrow
Let the record show
The stutters, waffle, and guff
Let the record show
How little we give a stuff
Let the record show
We cannot erase our past
How we gaslight and outcast
In real time
As the record shows.

Phone Atonement

I turn on my phone
And I start to zone
Out

Meaning to connect
But I'm starting to feel more alone
As I scroll through content
With no control
There's no room for content
In my heart or my soul
As I swipe through today's hype
                    today's gripes
                          side swipes and tripe.
My head feels numb
From other insights and insults
From humdrum to bots screaming scum
Pain throbs at my head
As I scroll through another never-ending thread.

I need to take stock
How on earth did I get here? About to press block
On Billie Pipers ex
It comes as a shock
You should care what he thinks
But we do
And it's not because we want to
                    it's not because we want to.

But I need to press block
On those who shock and mock
And to shake this feeling so hollow
I need to press unfollow
                unfollow

unfollow.

Opinions have become so absolute
There's no way back to nuance or making a moot
Point
In this app of increasingly ill repute
Where people are left free to persecute
I remember I can press   mute
                                mute
                                mute

And if I really don't like someone's tone
I consider putting down the phone
Put down the phone and go outside
And atone
For my time behind the screen
Get out and speak to someone real
And instantly realise how much better that makes
me feel.

Omission

They barely noticed
The word he chose to omit

All so well spoken and smartly dressed
We didn't even see when we began to commit
To his distortions
Hearing his verbal contortions.

Taking specific care to twist his verbs and joust
his nouns
Diverting and distracting, with such flair, such
charm
How could we notice, his decision of omission?

Soon it was just his sport
To dodge
That one word
Deleted

We see his version
Repeated and repeated
On tv transmissions
Distorting
With their further omissions

What was read and watched
Informed our view
So quickly, that we barely knew
The word that was never said

Again.

His choice to refrain from a mere detail

For his deliberate and selfish gain

To ensure we'd fail to see the facts
We needed before
His words split us into so many factions

Of those who noticed a flaw
And those who believed what they saw
The man before them, believing his word
Not seeing as yet more were redacted
People who questioned told they'd overreacted

Truth got lost in detail absent
Detailed neglect, designed to collect shares and
likes
Protection of wealth, shares and his stripes

Do they battle their conscience and all that
implies?
Do we even know who is the bad guy?
Their fear loss in the voting booth
Is so great that no one may ever see the real truth.

To the women

I can't share my stories

In solidarity

As my stories could unravel me

Not he

Who should unravel his misogyny

And learn how to be a better he.

Hashtags

Hashtags hashtags everywhere
And not much time to think
Hashtags hashtags everywhere
Nor a moment to shrink
We see how deep it does rot
And how we let it be
Our horror it has been too long
Eyes open we see
Hashtags hashtags everywhere
Creating and sharing links
Hashtags hashtags everywhere
Let's create a stink.

The death of decency

Decency dressed smartly that day
As they always did
Although their invitations were drying up
Decency now accused of being a mere signal
...Of virtue
Now apparently a bad thing.

Decency deceased they said
By gaslight
Empathy extinguished
Sympathy slayed
Disdain now reigned
Undaunted by humanity
Indecency was unrepentant
Removed from remorse
Goodwill, now, a ghost.

But charity inherited decency's clothes
So, charity challenged
Those troubled by truth
Ignored the insults
Honoured honesty
Demanded dignity
Charity lovingly dedicated to
Restoration of respectability.

Charity weaved decency into all it did
Let others try it on for size
Remembering how it feels to feel good
To help others feel good
Just felt good
A basic part of society's fabric
Never out of fashion

Or packed away
A mere statement or signal
A virtue worn with pride
Pride, that they don't let others fall.

Decency is in the details
The devil is in the drivel
Deluded drivel
Distorting drivel
Deceiving dodging drivel.

Decency keeping its own frequency
Reflects back drivel's deficiencies
Holding its own
Decency never rests
Decency never dies.

PART THREE
Haikus

Pride Haiku

Pride is self-assured
It does not dress in conceit
Stands alone, complete

Confidence Haiku

Confidence is calm
It is simply free from doubt
With no need to shout

PART FOUR
Lockdown Acrostics

During lockdown I would find myself scribbling down brief acrostics in response to the news that day.

It accumulated into this collection that instantly transport you back to pinpoint moments in time.

FaceTime

Far
Away.
Can't
Even
Touch.
I
Miss
Everything

News

Never
Ending
OverWhelming
Stream

Stay Alert

Slogans
That
Are
Yellow

And
Lime
Encourage a
Risk of
Trouble

Slogan

Stay alert
Lamb to the slaughter
Oven ready
Get mission done
Actions speak louder than words
Never forget
Stay at home

Yachts & planes

You
Actually
Can't
Honestly
Think

Painting
Literal
Aeroplanes
Negates
Everything?
Seriously?

Anger

A
New
Grown
Extraordinary
Rage

Systemic

So
You
Saw
Them
Evade?
Mislead?
Ignore?
Corrupt?

So
You
Should
Try
Encouraging
Making
Insisting on
CHANGE.

Silence

Should
I
Look
Elsewhere?
Never
Challenging
Establishment?

Osmosis

Orbiting
Statues
Many
Oafs
Safeguard
Imaginary
Significance

USA

Unbelievable
Scenes
Alarming

Home

Here
Our
Memories
Exist

Women

Women
Owe
Men
Exactly
Nothing

Kindness

Kindness
Is
Noticing
Demonstrating
Needed
Emotions
Saving
Souls

Bullying

But
Usually
Leaders
Like
You
Ignore
Negative
Grievances

Viable

Vivid
Imaginations
Authors, Actors
Brilliant breathtaking blockbusters, broadcasts and
books
Legitimate legacies
Essential economies

Tiers

Trouble
Is
Egos
Rarely
Save societies

Total
Incompetents
Exhaust
Reason &
Science

Too
Exhausted
And
Raging
Since
March now

LISA O'HARE

About The Author

Lisa O'Hare (she/her)

Lisa is based in north west England and started sharing her writing at spoken word events for the first time in 2019 after writing and performing a play at the Greater Manchester Fringe.

In 2020, like all of us, she had to take her life and words online, where she shared them on social media and across various zoom open mic events.

During this time, she focused on poetry writing and was published online by Visual Verse, Write Out Loud and Nymphs & Thugs. Lisa had poems featured in anthologies by Printed Words, The Black Engine Room Press and Local Gems Buzzin' Bards Anthology along with fundraising zines by the Coronaverses Collective and MadWomxn.

Lisa performs regularly at spoken word events such as Verbose, Speak Easy and Testify and has had two poems featured on BBC Radio Manchester's Upload hour, including the title poem, Lockdown Life a Rollercoaster of emotions. Cheshire East Libraries also featured the title poem in their National Poetry Day celebrations.

www.lisaoharewriter.com
Instagram & Twitter: @thelisaohare
YouTube: Lisa's Poetry Pages

Previous credits for poems in this collection

'Lockdown Life a Rollercoaster of emotions' – was originally written for a challenge set by Manchester based Two Time Theatre company on their Twitter account. It was subsequently featured by BBC Radio Manchester in their Upload show. Cheshire East Libraries posted the video of this poem on all their Facebook pages for National Poetry Day. It was also featured online by Inspiration in Isolation. The poem also featured on Some Good Ideas Lockdown Radio Podcast.

'Nonet for a world leader' and the 'Death of Decency' were published online by Nymphs & Thugs.

'Days Indistinguishable' was also originally written in response to a prompt by the Two Time Theatre company and was published online by 'Write Out Loud Poetry'.

'Calculating the R of Common Sense' and 'Mole Whacking' were included in issue two of the Coronaverses Collective magazine.

'A poem for Christmas 2020' won the Muddy Feet Poetry Christmas video on their YouTube channel.

'For The Women' was featured in UN Women UK Virtual Exhibition in April 2021 in conjunction with Poets Versus.

Lockdown Writers Block will be featured in Dear 2021 zine

Three poems from this collection were featured in an episode of the Alternative Stories and Fake Realities podcast

LISA O'HARE

' Me and my shadow on a lockdown walk'.

A self-portrait by Lisa O'Hare, as featured in 'You Are Here' online gallery by the Scottish National Gallery in 2020

MASTER HOUSE
Publishing

Independent press. Diverse inclusive writing,
stories & poetry from women of all backgrounds.
Focusing on new writing from emerging &
established women writers & those under-
served in mainstream publishing

www.masterhousepublishing.com

hello@masterhousepublishing.com

@masterhousepublishing

@masterhousepub

@masterhousepublish

MASTER HOUSE
Publishing

www.masterhousepublishing.com

Lightning Source UK Ltd.
Milton Keynes UK
UKHW010642310521
384676UK00002B/414

9 781838 482916